FAA Oversight of Procedures and Technologies toPrevent and Mitigate the Effects of Dense, Continuous Smoke in the Cockpit

June 4, 2013

The Honorable John D. Rockefeller
Chairman
The Honorable John Thune
Ranking Member
Committee on Commerce, Science, and Transportation
United States Senate

The Honorable Bill Shuster
Chairman
The Honorable Nick J. Rahall, II
Ranking Member
Committee on Transportation and Infrastructure
United States House of Representatives

Subject: *FAA Oversight of Procedures and Technologies to Prevent and Mitigate the Effects of Dense, Continuous Smoke in the Cockpit*

The FAA Modernization and Reform Act of 2012[1] directed the Comptroller General of the United States to conduct a study on the effectiveness of the Federal Aviation Administration's (FAA) oversight of the use of new technologies to prevent or mitigate the effects of dense, continuous smoke in the cockpit of commercial aircraft. FAA oversees these procedures and technologies as part of its mission to provide the safest, most efficient aerospace system. In the initial phase of our research, we determined that there was only one technology that was developed to specifically target dense, continuous smoke in the cockpit and that this type of event occurred so infrequently that it was not practical for us to evaluate the effectiveness of FAA's oversight.[2] However, we were able to identify relevant procedures that are more broadly targeted—for instance, at smoke, fire, or fume events.[3] Consistent with the mandate, we gathered stakeholders' views regarding the effectiveness of FAA's oversight of these procedures and the technologies related to preventing or mitigating the effects of dense, continuous smoke in the cockpit.

---

[1]Pub. L. No. 112-95, § 316, 126 Stat. 11, 69 (2012).

[2]The National Transportation Safety Board and FAA identified no accidents or incidents, respectively, occurring from 2002 through 2012, as involving dense, continuous smoke in the cockpit.

[3]We limited our consideration of "commercial aircraft" to those airplanes flown by air carriers offering scheduled, commercial service and operating under 14 C.F.R. Part 121.These include operations typically involving turbojet airplanes or any airplane with a seating capacity of more than nine passenger seats or a maximum payload capacity of more than 7,500 pounds.

After discussing this issue with your offices, we determined that the content and focus of this GAO study—how FAA oversees the limited number of procedures and technologies that prevent or mitigate the effects of dense, continuous smoke in the cockpit and stakeholders' views on the effectiveness of that oversight—is fully responsive to the GAO mandate contained in Section 316 of the FAA Modernization and Reform Act.

To identify how FAA oversees the use of relevant procedures and technologies, we reviewed FAA safety standards, guidance, and reports. To identify stakeholders' views on the effectiveness of FAA's oversight, we reviewed relevant National Transportation Safety Board (NTSB) recommendations and interviewed 15 stakeholders representing various sectors of the aviation community, including: officials from FAA and NTSB, representatives from pilots associations (Air Line Pilots Association and Coalition of Airline Pilots Associations), an air carrier trade association (Airlines for America), aircraft manufacturers (Boeing and Airbus), air carriers (United Parcel Service and JetBlue Airways), an aviation safety organization (Flight Safety Foundation), and a company that manufactures a device designed to mitigate the effects of dense, continuous smoke in the cockpit; and four aviation safety professionals. We selected these entities to represent a range of constituencies and perspectives. Safety professionals were identified based on conversations with other stakeholders. However, all stakeholders did not comment on the oversight of each identified procedure or technology. Moreover, their opinions are not generalizable to all aviation community stakeholders. To provide context for this study, we obtained the numbers of accidents and incidents from 2002 through 2012 that involved dense, continuous smoke in the cockpit identified by NTSB and FAA, respectively.[4,5] We interviewed the agency officials who generated the requested analyses and reviewed official documentation that accompanied the analyses. We determined that these numbers were sufficiently reliable for the descriptive analyses used in this report. We conducted this performance audit from September 2012 through May 2013 in accordance with generally accepted government auditing standards. Those standards require that we plan and perform the audit to obtain sufficient, appropriate evidence to provide a reasonable basis for our findings and conclusions based on our audit objectives. We believe that the evidence obtained provides a reasonable basis for our findings and conclusions based on our audit objectives.

Generally, FAA oversees the safety of commercial aviation by setting safety standards and conducting a range of activities to ensure compliance with those standards. These activities include: certifying airplane design and production, inspecting air carriers' and maintenance and repair facilities' operations, and licensing pilots and other personnel. FAA also conducts investigations following accidents and incidents, or in response to an apparent or alleged violation, and monitors safety-related data voluntarily reported by air carriers, pilots, airplane and parts manufacturers, maintenance personnel, and others. With regard to dense, continuous smoke in the cockpit, FAA's primary emphasis is on (1) preventing sources of ignition; (2) reducing the flammability of materials in the aircraft; (3) detecting and suppressing fires early; and (4) evacuating smoke from the cockpit.

---

[4]NTSB investigates and reports on civil aviation accidents, which it defines as occurrences whereby a person suffers death or serious injury, or in which the aircraft receives substantial damage. FAA and NTSB also investigate aviation incidents, which NTSB defines as occurrences other than an accident associated with the operation of an aircraft that affects or could affect the safety of operations.

[5]Neither NTSB nor FAA tracks the occurrence of dense, continuous smoke, and a definitive determination could not be made for some events.

In summary, FAA uses a variety of approaches, including certifying airplane design and inspecting air carriers, to oversee procedures and technologies that prevent or mitigate the effects of dense, continuous smoke in the cockpit. In the course of our review, we identified five such procedures and technologies that FAA oversees. They are:

- *Evacuation of dense smoke from the cockpit*—FAA's certification standards for aircraft design include that smoke evacuation must be readily accomplished. Additionally, FAA's guidelines state that airplane manufacturers may demonstrate compliance with this requirement by evacuating dense smoke from the cockpit within 3 minutes. The guidelines also recommend, but do not require, that manufacturers demonstrate the capability to evacuate continuously generated smoke from the cockpit. However, according to FAA, no manufacturer has yet chosen to demonstrate this capability.

- *Protective breathing equipment for the flightcrew*—FAA requires air carriers to provide protective breathing equipment that protects the flightcrew from the effects of smoke. The equipment must supply breathing gas for at least 15 minutes, must allow the pilots to use communication equipment, and must be readily accessible by the pilot. FAA inspections of aircraft include checks of this equipment.

- *Pilot training on emergency procedures*—FAA requires air carriers' pilot training programs to cover principles of emergency operations and emergency communications procedures. Specific to in-flight smoke and fire situations, FAA recommends that air carriers' training programs ensure that flight crewmembers understand the potential effects of the airplane's ventilation systems on hidden fires and that pilots practice planning for an immediate descent and landing at the nearest suitable airport. FAA approves air carriers' training program curricula and conducts periodic inspections.

- *Checklist to respond to smoke in the cockpit*—FAA requires that an FAA-approved checklist that includes emergency procedures be provided by air carriers and used by their flight crewmembers. FAA conducts periodic inspections related to these requirements. In addition, FAA participated in an industry-led effort to develop a smoke, fire, and fumes checklist template and recommendations related to its use. FAA recommends, but does not require, that an air carrier's relevant parties (e.g., directors of safety and pilots) collaborate to consider applying these documents in their related checklists.

- *Emergency Vision Assurance System (EVAS)*—EVAS consists of an inflatable transparent unit that provides the pilot with a "window" to view their instruments and out the windshield when there is dense, continuous smoke in the cockpit. FAA has approved the installation of the device for several models of commercial airplanes. FAA evaluated EVAS and concluded that EVAS does not provide a significant safety benefit and the potential benefits of EVAS do not warrant the costs that would be incurred by industry if FAA were to mandate installation because (1) dense, continuous smoke in the cockpit is a very rare event and (2) accidents in which dense, continuous smoke has occurred indicate that according to FAA, such scenarios "are likely to be catastrophic for reasons other than flightcrew visibility (e.g., loss of airplane controllability, structural failure)." Further, dense, continuous smoke in the cockpit has only once been identified by NTSB as a cause of a commercial aviation accident.[6]

For three of these procedures and technologies, the stakeholders we interviewed generally agreed that FAA's oversight was effective or sufficient; for the remaining two, the stakeholders had mixed views about the effectiveness of FAA's oversight. The stakeholders generally agreed that FAA's oversight of protective breathing equipment, pilot training, and cockpit checklists was effective. NTSB has made recommendations related to these procedures and technologies—for example, that FAA require air carriers to include, as the first step in their checklists, that flight crewmembers don their oxygen masks and verify that they are set to supply 100 percent oxygen (Recommendation A-11-91). FAA is in the process of responding to NTSB on these recommendations. With regard to FAA's oversight of the evacuation of dense smoke from the cockpit and EVAS, stakeholders had mixed views. For instance, some stakeholders—including the manufacturer of EVAS—said that FAA should start requiring manufacturers to (1) demonstrate the capability to evacuate dense, continuous smoke from the cockpit or (2) install a device such as EVAS that would enable the pilot to continue to navigate the airplane with dense, continuous smoke in the cockpit. Other stakeholders said that FAA's oversight related to smoke evacuation and EVAS was sufficient. They said that FAA should not require manufacturers to demonstrate the capability to evacuate dense, continuous smoke from the cockpit because such smoke occurs so infrequently. Stakeholders that said FAA's oversight was sufficient generally agreed with its rationale for not mandating the installation of EVAS. See the enclosure for additional details of our findings.

We provided DOT and NTSB with a draft of this report for their review and comment. DOT generally agreed with the report and NTSB provided technical comments that we incorporated as appropriate.

We are sending copies of this report to the appropriate congressional committees, the Secretary of Transportation, and the Chairman of NTSB. This report will also be available at no charge on the GAO website at http://www.gao.gov. Should you or your staff have questions concerning this report, please contact me at (202) 512-2834 or dillinghamg@gao.gov. Contact points for our Offices of Congressional Relations and Public Affairs may be found on the last page of this report. Key contributors to this report were Heather MacLeod (Assistant Director), Melissa Bodeau, Russ Burnett, Leia Dickerson, David Goldstein, Bert Japikse, Josh Ormond, and Jessica Wintfeld.

Gerald L. Dillingham, Ph.D.
Director
Physical Infrastructure Issues

Enclosure

---

[6]On November 3, 1973, Pan American World Airways, Inc., Clipper Flight 160, a Boeing 707-321C (N458PA) crashed at Logan International Airport, Boston, Massachusetts. NTSB determined that the probable cause of the accident was the presence of smoke, which was continuously generated and uncontrollable, in the cockpit. However, according to FAA, even under these conditions, the NTSB does not state that the airplane crashed because the crew could not see the ground or instruments. The airplane was on final approach when control problems related to loss of electrical power caused it to stall and impact the ground.

FAA's Oversight of Technologies that Prevent or Mitigate the Effects of Dense, Continuous Smoke in the Cockpit

Mandated by Section 316, FAA Modernization and Reform Act of 2012 (Pub. L. No.112-95)

For more information, contact Dr. Gerald Dillingham, dillinghamg@gao.gov   Page 1

Mandate

Section 316, FAA Modernization and Reform Act of 2012 directed the Comptroller General of the United States to conduct a study on the effectiveness of the Federal Aviation Administration's (FAA) oversight of the use of new technologies to prevent or mitigate the effects of dense, continuous smoke in the cockpit of a commercial aircraft (Pub. L. No.112-95, § 316, 126 Stat. 11, 69).

GAO

Objective

This report addresses how FAA oversees the limited number of procedures and technologies that prevent or mitigate the effects of dense, continuous smoke in the cockpit, and stakeholders' views on the effectiveness of that oversight.

- We gathered stakeholders' views regarding the effectiveness of FAA's oversight of procedures and technologies directly related to dense, continuous smoke in the cockpit, but did not evaluate FAA's oversight mechanisms.

- We determined that there was only one technology that was developed to specifically target dense, continuous smoke in the cockpit and that this type of event occurred so infrequently that it was not practical for us to evaluate the effectiveness of FAA's oversight.

GAO

Scope of Work

- We identified procedures and technologies that prevent or mitigate the effects of smoke already in the cockpit.

- We limited our consideration of "commercial aircraft" to those airplanes flown by air carriers offering scheduled, commercial service and operating under 14 C.F.R. Part 121. These typically include operations involving turbojet airplanes or airplanes with a seating capacity of more than nine passenger seats or a maximum payload capacity of more than 7,500 pounds.

Page 4

GAO

Methods

- We reviewed FAA safety standards, guidance, and reports; National Transportation Safety Board (NTSB) recommendations; and relevant literature.

- We interviewed 15 stakeholders representing various sectors of the aviation community, including: officials from FAA and NTSB; representatives from pilots associations (Air Line Pilots Association and Coalition of Airline Pilots Associations), an air carrier trade association (Airlines for America), aircraft manufacturers (Boeing and Airbus), air carriers (United Parcel Service and JetBlue Airways), an aviation safety organization (Flight Safety Foundation), and a company that manufactures a device designed to mitigate the effects of dense, continuous smoke in the cockpit; and four aviation safety professionals.

- We selected these entities to represent a range of constituencies and perspectives. Safety professionals were identified based on conversations with other stakeholders.

- All stakeholders did not comment on the oversight of each identified procedure or technology. Moreover, their opinions are not generalizable to all aviation stakeholders.

GAO

Methods, continued

- We obtained the numbers of accidents and incidents from 2002 through 2012 identified by NTSB and FAA, respectively, as involving dense, continuous smoke in the cockpit.

- Neither agency tracks the occurrence of dense, continuous smoke, and a definitive determination could not be made for some events.

- We interviewed the agency officials who generated the requested analyses and reviewed official documentation that accompanied the analyses. We determined that these numbers were sufficiently reliable for the descriptive analyses used in this report.

Page 6

GAO

Background: Definition of *Dense, Continuous Smoke*

- Neither FAA nor NTSB has formally defined *dense, continuous smoke*.

- FAA and NTSB generally agree that *dense smoke* is smoke that prevents a pilot from seeing the flight controls.

- Based on FAA guidance, we defined *continuous smoke* as smoke that continues to enter the cockpit for some time after it reaches the level of dense smoke.

Background: Sources of Dense, Continuous Smoke in the Cockpit

Dense, continuous smoke can occur in the cockpit due primarily to

- a fire in the cockpit or
- a fire in another part of the plane, such as a cargo compartment.

GAO

Background: Dense, Continuous Smoke in the Cockpit Events from 2002 through 2012

While FAA receives several reports a year of smoke in the cockpit of commercial airplanes, dense, continuous smoke has been reported infrequently.

- NTSB and FAA identified no accidents or incidents, respectively, occurring from 2002 through 2012 as involving dense, continuous smoke in the cockpit.

  - Dense, continuous smoke, and the inability to see as a result, have been identified once by NTSB as a cause of an aviation accident (Pan American World Airways Flight 160, a cargo flight, in 1973).

Page 9

GAO

Background: FAA's Oversight of Aviation Safety

- FAA oversees the safety of commercial aviation by setting safety standards and conducting a range of activities to ensure compliance with those standards. These activities include:
  - certifying airplane design and production,
  - inspecting air carriers' and maintenance and repair facilities' operations, and
  - licensing pilots and other personnel.
- FAA also
  - conducts investigations following accidents and incidents, or in response to an apparent or alleged violation and
  - monitors safety-related data voluntarily reported by air carriers, pilots, airplane and parts manufacturers, maintenance personnel, and others.

Page 10

GAO

Background: FAA's Approach to Address Dense, Continuous Smoke in the Cockpit

FAA's primary emphasis is on:

- preventing sources of ignition,
- reducing the flammability of materials in the aircraft,
- detecting and suppressing fires early, and
- evacuating smoke from the cockpit.

FAA Uses a Variety of Approaches to Oversee Procedures and Technologies that Prevent or Mitigate the Effects of Dense, Continuous Smoke in the Cockpit

- FAA sets standards and conducts tests or inspections related to:
  - airplane capability to evacuate smoke from the cockpit,
  - protective breathing equipment for pilots, and
  - training of pilots on emergency procedures.
- FAA has issued guidance related to air carriers' use of an industry-developed emergency procedure checklist.
- FAA has approved installation, for several airplane models, of the Emergency Vision Assurance System (EVAS), a device designed to maintain pilots' view of flight instruments and out the windshield in dense, continuous smoke conditions.
- For three of these procedures and technologies, the stakeholders we interviewed generally agreed that FAA's oversight was effective or sufficient; for the remaining two, the stakeholders had mixed views about the effectiveness of FAA's oversight.

GAO

FAA Requires that Airplanes Be Able to Evacuate Dense Smoke from the Cockpit

- FAA's certification standards for aircraft design include that "if accumulation of hazardous quantities of smoke in the cockpit area is reasonably probable, smoke evacuation must be readily accomplished, starting with full pressurization and without depressurizing beyond safe limits" (14 C.F.R. § 25.831(d)).

- FAA's guidelines describe the following test procedure that manufacturers may use to demonstrate compliance with this standard (Advisory Circular 25-9A).

  - Smoke should be generated until "the cockpit instruments are obscured [i.e., there is dense smoke in the cockpit] ..." at which point "smoke generation should be terminated, and ... fire and smoke procedures should be initiated. The smoke should be reduced within three minutes such that any residual smoke (haze) does not distract the flightcrew or interfere with flight operations."

Page 13

GAO

FAA Requires that Airplanes Be Able to Evacuate Dense Smoke from the Cockpit, continued

- According to FAA, airplane manufacturers generally meet FAA's smoke evacuation standard by using the airplane's ventilation system to increase the flow of fresh air from outside the airplane into the cockpit, forcing the smoke out.

- FAA's guidelines also recommend, but do not require, manufacturers to demonstrate the capability to evacuate *continuously generated* smoke from the cockpit.

  - According to FAA, no manufacturer has yet chosen to demonstrate this capability.

Page 14

Stakeholders Interviewed Have Mixed Views about the Effectiveness of FAA's Smoke Evacuation Standard

Some stakeholders believe that FAA's smoke evacuation standard is effective.

- Some of these stakeholders stated that—given the very small likelihood of a dense, continuous smoke event—it is reasonable for FAA's current test procedure to call for termination of smoke generation when cockpit instruments are obscured.

Stakeholders Interviewed Have Mixed Views about the Effectiveness of FAA's Smoke Evacuation Standard, continued

- Other stakeholders stated that:

  - FAA's above-mentioned test procedure—because it calls for terminating smoke generation when the cockpit instruments are obscured—is unrealistic,

  - FAA should revise its test procedure to require evacuation of dense, *continuous* smoke, and

  - FAA should require manufacturers to either (1) demonstrate the capability to evacuate dense, continuous smoke or (2) provide equipment, such as EVAS, to maintain pilots' view of flight instruments and out the windshield in dense, continuous smoke conditions.

Page 16

FAA Requires Air Carriers to Equip Their Airplanes with Protective Breathing Equipment for Pilots

- FAA requires air carriers to furnish protective breathing equipment that protects the flightcrew from the effects of smoke, carbon dioxide, or other harmful gases or an oxygen deficient environment. The equipment must (14 C.F.R. § 121.337):
  - allow use of communication equipment and must not impair vision to the extent that duties cannot be accomplished,
  - be conveniently located in the cockpit for immediate use by the crewmember at his or her duty station, and
  - supply breathing gas for at least 15 minutes.
- Air carriers equip their airplanes with either separate oxygen masks and goggles or full-face masks with combined oxygen and eye protection.
- FAA's periodic inspections of airplanes include checks of this equipment.

Page 17

GAO-13-551R Smoke in the Cockpit

GAO

Almost All Stakeholders Interviewed Prefer Full-Face Oxygen Mask

Almost all stakeholders we interviewed prefer the full-face mask to the separate oxygen mask and goggles because it is easier to don and more comfortable for pilots.

Figure 1: Demonstration of Donning a Full-Face Mask that Combines Oxygen Delivery and Eye Protection

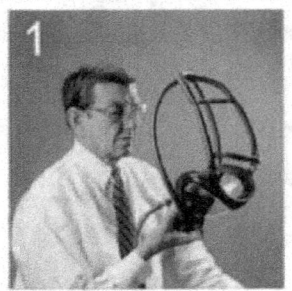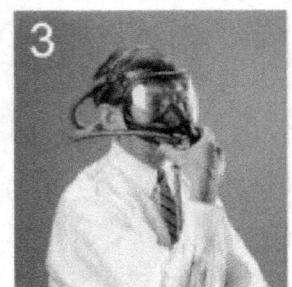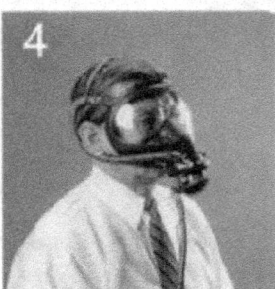

©2013 B/E Aerospace. Inc.

Most Stakeholders Interviewed Find FAA's Oversight of Protective Breathing Equipment for Pilots to be Effective

- Most stakeholders we interviewed are satisfied with FAA's oversight of protective breathing equipment for use in conditions of dense, continuous smoke in the cockpit.

- Despite their preference for the full-face mask, most stakeholders said that FAA should not require air carriers to install it because they believe that industry is largely adopting the full-face mask on its own.

- NTSB recommended that FAA require installation of the full-face oxygen mask (Recommendation A-11-87). According to NTSB, the full-face oxygen masks are easier to don, adjust, and use than separate oxygen masks and goggles.

  - FAA reviewed accident and incident data and found a lack of events where the crew's inability to secure their oxygen masks may have played a role in the outcome of the event. As a result, it decided not to require installation of the full-face oxygen mask. NTSB has not yet responded to FAA's decision.

Page 19

GAO

FAA Sets Standards for Air Carriers' Training of Pilots on Emergency Procedures

FAA requires air carriers' pilot training programs to cover principles of emergency operations and each emergency procedure for each type of airplane. Training programs must also cover emergency communication procedures (14 C.F.R. § 121.419).

- FAA approves air carriers' training program curricula and FAA conducts periodic inspections to ensure compliance with these requirements.

GAO

FAA Sets Standards for Air Carriers' Training of Pilots on Emergency Procedures, continued

- Specific to in-flight smoke and fire situations, FAA recommends that operator's training programs ensure that flight crewmembers (Advisory Circular 120-80):

  - understand the airplane's ventilation systems with emphasis on the potential effects of airflow on hidden fires; and

  - practice procedures associated with planning for an immediate descent and landing at the nearest suitable airport, operating the airplane with the use of protective breathing equipment and smoke goggles, and means of dispersing smoke and fumes when the source of a fire is unknown.

- Air carriers train their pilots in these areas using classroom training or a combination of classroom and flight simulator training.

Most Stakeholders Interviewed Said that FAA's Oversight of Pilot Training on Emergency Procedures is Sufficient

- Most stakeholders we interviewed said that FAA's oversight of pilot training on emergency procedures is sufficient.

- However, NTSB made several recommendations related to the training for and use of oxygen masks (Recommendations A-11-88 through -90). NTSB recommended that:

  - FAA require air carriers provide pilots hands-on training regarding the donning and operation of oxygen masks and goggles during initial and recurrent training.

  - FAA require air carriers to provide pilots training on maintaining cockpit communications when oxygen masks are donned.

  - FAA require air carriers to educate pilots on the importance of stowing their oxygen masks set to supply 100 percent oxygen. NTSB found on long cargo flights, pilots may leave the cockpit for breaks during which they may use their oxygen mask set to normal rather than 100 percent, creating opportunities for stowing the mask set to normal and, thus, not in a ready setting for a smoke, fire, or fumes event.

- FAA responded to NTSB with its intention to address these recommendations by revising its guidance (Advisory Circular 120-80) and plans to publish the update by June 2014.

FAA Requires an FAA-Approved Checklist that Includes Emergency Procedures

FAA requires that an FAA-approved checklist that includes emergency procedures be provided by air carriers for use by their flight crewmembers (14 C.F.R. § 121.315).

- FAA conducts periodic inspections related to these requirements.

FAA Participated in the Development of and Issued Guidance Related to Air Carriers' Use of a Checklist Template for Smoke and Fire Emergencies

- FAA participated in an effort undertaken by airplane manufacturers, air carriers, professional pilots associations, and other industry specialists to produce an in-flight smoke, fire, and fumes checklist template and recommendations related to its use.

- FAA recommends, but does not require, that an air carrier's relevant parties (e.g., directors of safety and pilots) be aware of these documents and consider collaborating to apply them to their own checklists (Information for Operators 08034).

- Some stakeholders we interviewed said that the checklist template has been adopted by manufacturers and air carriers.

GAO

Most Stakeholders Interviewed Are Satisfied with FAA's Oversight of Checklists for Smoke and Fire Emergencies

- Most stakeholders said that the current oversight is sufficient.
- Other stakeholders said that
    - FAA should require use of the checklist template;
    - FAA should include the template in its guidance on smoke and fire emergencies; or
    - FAA should collaboratively develop a separate checklist specifically for dense, continuous smoke in the cockpit.

Page 25

Most Stakeholders Interviewed Are Satisfied with FAA's Oversight of Checklists for Smoke and Fire Emergencies, continued

- NTSB recommended FAA require air carriers to include, as the first step in their checklists, that flight crewmembers don their oxygen masks and verify that they are set to supply 100 percent oxygen (Recommendation A-11-91). This recommendation is the result of an ongoing accident investigation where NTSB found that the emergency checklists of the carrier involved in the accident did not follow the template and recommendations for use, which call for flight crews to ensure oxygen masks and goggles are donned and properly set immediately after smoke, fire, or fumes detection.

- FAA responded to NTSB with its intention to address these recommendations and subsequently told us that it plans to update its guidance by late 2014 or 2015.

GAO

FAA Has Approved the Installation of EVAS for Several Airplane Models

- EVAS is designed to maintain pilots' view in dense, continuous smoke conditions.

- It consists of a battery-powered blower that filters visible particles out of the air and pumps the filtered air into an inflatable transparent unit that provides the pilot with a "window" to view their instruments and out the windshield.

- It has been installed on airplanes flown by passenger carrier JetBlue and cargo carrier Kalitta Air; cargo carriers United Parcel Service and FedEx plan to install it.

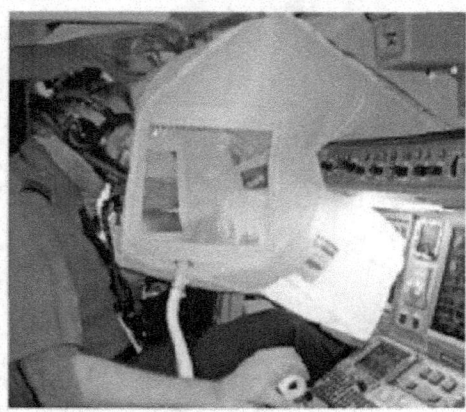

©2007 VisionSafe Corporation

Page 27

GAO

FAA Decided Not to Mandate the Installation of EVAS

FAA evaluated EVAS and concluded that the potential benefits of EVAS do not warrant the costs that would be incurred by industry if FAA were to mandate installation. According to FAA:

- EVAS does not provide a significant safety benefit because:
  - dense, continuous smoke in the cockpit that cannot be safely evacuated by normal means is a very rare event, and
  - accidents in which dense, continuous smoke has occurred indicate that such scenarios "are likely to be catastrophic for reasons other than flightcrew visibility (e.g., loss of airplane controllability, structural failure)."
- Unnecessary deployment of EVAS may actually decrease safety because it could impede other crew actions.

GAO

Stakeholders Interviewed Have Mixed Views about the Effectiveness of FAA's Oversight of EVAS

- Some stakeholders said that FAA's oversight is sufficient because they believe that the costs of installing the system outweigh the benefits.

- Other stakeholders—including the manufacturer of EVAS—said that the benefits of installation outweigh the costs.

    - These stakeholders believe that in the accidents where dense, continuous smoke occurred in the cockpit, the smoke was a cause of the accident, specifically as it related to the pilot's inability to see to control the airplane—even in the cases in which NTSB determined that dense, continuous smoke in the cockpit was not a cause.

    - They believe that EVAS could have saved lives in those instances and, as a result, has benefits that are not being considered.

Page 29

Stakeholders Interviewed Have Mixed Views about the Effectiveness of FAA's Oversight of EVAS, continued

- NTSB recommended that FAA evaluate EVAS and take action as appropriate (Recommendation A-97-61). In 1996, NTSB noted that emergency vision technology existed and may be applicable in the event of smoke in the cockpit.

    - In response, FAA noted that it had already evaluated EVAS and determined that it is not necessary or appropriate to mandate installation of the system.

    - NTSB closed the recommendation noting that FAA's action complied with the recommendation to evaluate EVAS.

Page 30

GAO on the Web
Web site: http://www.gao.gov/

Congressional Relations
Katherine Siggerud, Managing Director, siggerudk@gao.gov
(202) 512-4400, U.S. Government Accountability Office
441 G Street, NW, Room 7125, Washington, DC 20548

Public Affairs
Chuck Young, Managing Director, youngc1@gao.gov
(202) 512-4800, U.S. Government Accountability Office
441 G Street, NW, Room 7149, Washington, DC 20548

(540243)

GAO's Mission	The Government Accountability Office, the audit, evaluation, and investigative arm of Congress, exists to support Congress in meeting its constitutional responsibilities and to help improve the performance and accountability of the federal government for the American people. GAO examines the use of public funds; evaluates federal programs and policies; and provides analyses, recommendations, and other assistance to help Congress make informed oversight, policy, and funding decisions. GAO's commitment to good government is reflected in its core values of accountability, integrity, and reliability.
Obtaining Copies of GAO Reports and Testimony	The fastest and easiest way to obtain copies of GAO documents at no cost is through GAO's website (www.gao.gov). Each weekday afternoon, GAO posts on its website newly released reports, testimony, and correspondence. To have GAO e-mail you a list of newly posted products, go to www.gao.gov and select "E-mail Updates."
Order by Phone	The price of each GAO publication reflects GAO's actual cost of production and distribution and depends on the number of pages in the publication and whether the publication is printed in color or black and white. Pricing and ordering information is posted on GAO's website, http://www.gao.gov/ordering.htm. Place orders by calling (202) 512-6000, toll free (866) 801-7077, or TDD (202) 512-2537. Orders may be paid for using American Express, Discover Card, MasterCard, Visa, check, or money order. Call for additional information.
Connect with GAO	Connect with GAO on Facebook, Flickr, Twitter, and YouTube. Subscribe to our RSS Feeds or E-mail Updates. Listen to our Podcasts. Visit GAO on the web at www.gao.gov.
To Report Fraud, Waste, and Abuse in Federal Programs	Contact: Website: www.gao.gov/fraudnet/fraudnet.htm E-mail: fraudnet@gao.gov Automated answering system: (800) 424-5454 or (202) 512-7470
Congressional Relations	Katherine Siggerud, Managing Director, siggerudk@gao.gov, (202) 512-4400, U.S. Government Accountability Office, 441 G Street NW, Room 7125, Washington, DC 20548
Public Affairs	Chuck Young, Managing Director, youngc1@gao.gov, (202) 512-4800 U.S. Government Accountability Office, 441 G Street NW, Room 7149 Washington, DC 20548